STORE FRONTS
ELMIRA, NEW YORK

by Diane Janowski

New York History Review
Elmira New York

Store Fronts - Elmira, New York
by Diane Janowski
Copyright © 2010 & 2022
New York History Review, Elmira, New York

Notice of Rights. All rights reserved. No part of this book may be reproduced or transmitted in any form by any means, electronic, mechanical, photocopying, recording or otherwise, without the prior written permission of the author. For more information on getting permission for reprints and excerpts, contact us through our website.
www.NewYorkHistoryReview.com

Second edition
ISBN: 978-1-950822-03-4

Printed in the United States of America

*A collection of beautiful old photographs
of commercial store fronts in Elmira, New York*

Elmira's neighborhood store fronts had the city's history etched in their facades. Most are gone but a few remain today. Each store was as unique as the customers they served and were run by owners who shared a commitment to provide a special service. Many shops were lifelines for their communities, vital to the residents who depended on them for a multitude of needs. Yet such shops disappeared as their neighborhoods and technology changed. Elmira and Chemung County still have a few humble neighborhood stores tucked away on narrow side streets but many have given way to well-known institutions on busy thoroughfares.

Through these old portraits of individual store fronts, this photography book reveals how neighborhood stores helped set the pulse, life, and texture of Elmira, New York at the turn of the 20th century.

For Constantine & Bill
- old friends -

Thank you

Stan & Linda Burnham
for donating many of these photographs
to the Eleanor Barnes Library

Table of Contents

image	page
Rossi's shoe store	9
Cary's cigar store	11
EWL&R Gas Stoves	13
Miller's butcher shop	15
Susemihl's barber shop	17
Fancy Goods	19
Pettit's drug store	21
Lawrence's candy	23
Leather Glove Company	25
Wagonmaker	27
Cooklin's saloon	29
Deister's grocery store	31
Baldwin Street	33
Bantley's wire works	35
Lunch parlor	37
Fritsch's grocery store	39
Windsor Hotel and lunch room	41
West Water Street	43
Church and Main Streets	45
Vinton's wines & liquors	47
Janowski's produce	49

Domenico Rossi's shoe store at 163 Railroad Avenue.

D. ROSSI,
LIST OF PRICES
MENS
SEWED SOLES & HEELS 80
SOLES 65
NAILED SOLES & HEELS 55
HEELS 20
SOLES 40
LADIES
SEWED SOLE & HEELS 65
"SOLES" 50
NAILED SOLES & HEEL 40
"SOLES" 30
CHILDRENS
NAILED SOLE & HEEL 30
"SOLES" 20
COME IN AND GIVE
A TRIAL AND BE CONVINCED

Azariah R. Cary's Cigar Store at 205 West Water Street.

Elmira Water, Light & Railroad's Gas Stove & Gas Appliance store, 154-156 Baldwin Street. Note the pile of coal in the window. On the left was Roll's Paint Store at 158 Baldwin Street.

William H. Miller's butcher shop at 561 East Church Street.

Robert Susemihl's barber shop at 145 West Water Street. The back of the photograph says "the cop's name is Hugo."

At a resolution of 2400 dpi we found the photographer's reflection above the second man from the left. It was an unexpected treat.

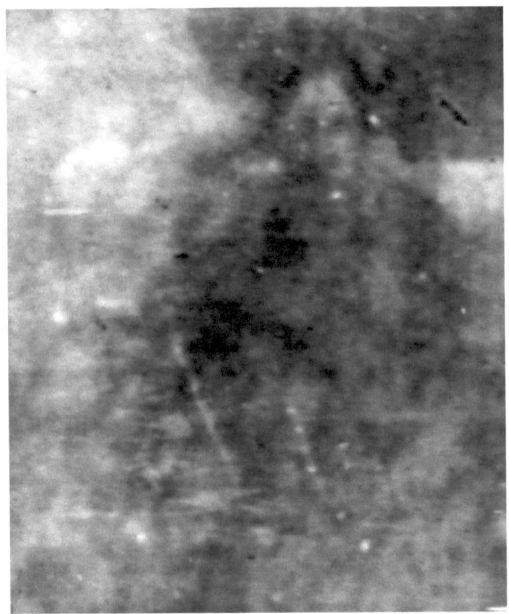

Uncertain, but possibly Alcesta Cook's Fancy Goods & Furnishings store, 114 North Main Street.

Charles P. Pettit's drug store at 116 North Main Street. Building still exists.

Thomas Lawrence's candy store at 138 West Water Street.

The Leather Glove Company at 121 East Church Street was owned by Arthur M. Northrup and Ernest J. Ketchum.

Uncertain, but possibly George Broas's wagonmaking business at 110 East Church.

Thomas Cooklin's saloon at 202 South Main Street. On the left is James Breger's barber shop.

John Deister's grocery store at 801 East Church Street.

Baldwin Street looking south. The big building on the right was the Rathbun Hotel. Some buildings still exist.

Constantine Bantley's Wire Works on the northwest corner of Madison Avenue and East Fifth Street. Mr. Bantley is on the top right. This building still exists.

Uncertain, but possibly Emma Shidlen's Lunch Parlor at 132 East Water Street.

The Fritch grocery store at the corner of Fourteenth Street and College Avenue in Elmira Heights. The building still exists.

The Windsor Quick Lunch and Hotel at 507-509 Railroad Avenue was owned by Michael J. Clohessy. At 509 was Ralph Murphy's lunch room.

Store fronts on West Water Street. Postcard publisher C.S. Woolworth, Elmira, NY.

Corner of East Church and State Streets looking north. On the corner is Frank Allen's painting company. Henry Heine and Edward Bauer ran an upholstery business. In the distance is the C.M.&R. Tompkins building. They roasted and packaged their own brand of coffee.

Charles E. Vinton's Wines & Liquors store at 102 Market Street.

The Janowski Brothers sold their special celery all over New York and Pennsylvania. Their store front was at 517 Esty Street. Building and business still exists.

More books from New York History Review

A Short and Sweet History of the Chemung Valley

The Park Church Souvenir Cookbook of 1906

The Great Inter-State Fair

Zim's Foolish History of Elmira

Zim's Foolish History of Horseheads

Frederick Douglass' Speech at Elmira

In Their Honor

In Dairyland

The True Stories series

A Brief History of Chemung County

Cartoons and Caricatures

Our Own Book

The Elmira Prison Camp